British Library Cataloguing Publication Data

ISBN 978-0-9544678-2-1

Publisher
Chris Marsh Publishing
94 Manor Green Road
Epsom, Surrey
KT19 8LN
England

The Baron in the Shower

And Other Poems

Compiled by

Liz Brown

Contents

Section 4 – School Friends 59-81

List of Illustrations

Introduction

I first met Richard Norman Cole, in 1973, when I was a little girl of seven. It was not until some years later, when I attended the Mary Hare Grammar School in 1977, the same year as Richard left, that I discovered just how popular and charming the young man was. The bonding has become so strong that some have never lost touch with their classmates some 30-odd years later.

In March 2006, in the days of improved internet technology, I stumbled across the old Yahoo 'Mary Hare' forum e-group. It was amazing to swap posts between forumites (members of the forum). Needless to say, Richard, who is very passionate about his beloved school, was also a forumite, and he wasted no time introducing me to the rest of the forum. It felt like home from home with many experiences to share between ourselves.

A discussion thread came up as to who the first person was to change their name by deed poll. Richard jokingly called himself the 'Baron Ricardo Claude Von Floppenstappen' and the nickname stuck! Within a few days, in July 2006, a new forum called the Mary Hare History Forum (MHHF) evolved, and forumites played along to a virtual story about the Baron and his virtual Cole Castle, based in Milton Keynes with his beloved 'sea gulls' hovering around. For the benefit of those who are not familiar, Richard is an avid Torquay United supporter (otherwise known as the 'Gulls').

In September 2006, I posted a humorous poem in relation to a topical theme about Richard literally breaking his leg in three places and being hospitalised for a few days. Over the next few weeks, I posted a few more poems about other topical themes. It quickly descended into a limerick competition.

In November 2006, everybody connected to Richard was devastated to hear that he was diagnosed as terminally ill with Motor Neurone Disease (MND). His work colleagues, friends and family wasted no time in starting fundraising different activities to raise awareness which enabled Richard and his wife, Jane, to obtain funding from their local MNDA branch in Milton Keynes. The money collected via Motor Neurone Disease Association allowed them to convert their house into a more disabled-friendly home.

In February 2007, Richard, with all due credit to him, managed to organise "a bit of a Mary Hare do" reunion for the former pupils from the 1970's decade, give or take a few others from earlier decades. He tracked down over 250, bringing together many former pupils, who had lost contact with their schoolmates, and in the process, raised a huge sum of money for the Mary Hare Foundation and the Motor Neurone Disease Association. To Richard's delight, the "Cole's Diner", a 1950s American-style diner, named after him, located in the basement of Mansell House (the boys' living quarters) at Mary Hare, has recently undergone a refurbishment and was officially opened on 30th September 2007. The Cole family and few private guests were invited to this special occasion.

Prior to my joining the Mary Hare History forum, I had no interest whatsoever in writing poetry. By accident, posting a poem as a one-off capitulated me into the limelight to be nicknamed the 'humorous resident poet' on the forum. Someone suggested I wrote a book of poems. I later started to come round to that idea and felt compelled to get into the spirit of fundraising myself and dedicate a book of poems to Richard.

I set myself a target to reach 100 poems to enable a wide variety of themes to reach a broader spectrum of readers. This was achieved with the advice and input of a few friends, who were more than willing to help out with their own poetry.

Most of the poems in this book are written by former pupils who attended the Mary Hare Grammar School in the 1960s-1980s. Some of their families also contributed their thoughts. Poems are mainly related to school life experiences, teachers, school events, and topical themes from the Mary Hare History Forum. A few other poems have been selected and reprinted from previous editions of *The Bluebird*, the school's own magazine published between the years 1970-1979. The proceeds from the book sale will be split equally between the Motor Neurone Disease Association, the Mary Hare Foundation, and the National Deaf Children's Society.

Andrea Fisher's poem asks of us a question that we all need to give answer to irrespective of which school we went to or what illness or disability we suffer from.

I would like to extend my grateful thanks to all those former pupils and their families for their encouragement, support and contributions to enable me to compile a book of poems, which is dedicated to Richard Norman Cole, our very dear friend, hence the opening title of the book is aptly named 'The Baron in the Shower!'

Liz Brown

Street, Somerset
September 2007

Richard Norman Cole and his guide dog, Robert

Acknowledgements

I would like to acknowledge the contributions of the following:

Mags Adams-Aston, for her wonderful illustrations.

Christine Kerr, for proof reading the contents of this book.

Ken Pearce, the school Principal during Richard's and my time at Mary Hare, who very kindly agreed to write the Foreword for the book.

Doctor David and Mrs Barbara Mazey for their kind permission to include the poem 'Me', by the late Anne Mazey. Anne, a former pupil from Mary Hare also suffered from motor neurone disease.

Meg Hardman, for permission to reprint the late Michael's poem

Elaine Lavery, for her advice, encouragement and direction.

Christopher Marsh, for printing and publication of this book.

To all those wannabe poets named in this book who voluntarily gave some of their time to write a bit of poetry.

My special thanks also go to Alison Cookson (née Mayer), who had contributed a significant number of her poems.

Judith Anderson (née Shaw), for the concept of using her poem to give the book its title.

Finally, a special thank you to the reader, for purchasing this book, and raising worthwhile funds for a good cause.

Foreword

Anne Mazey was a remarkable young woman. She was brave, constant, strong in determination but what, in my experience, was the most remarkable characteristic she possessed was serenity. It is a characteristic which every one of us would want to possess but few of us genuinely achieve and it is the reason why I shall never forget Anne. It is fitting that she should be remembered in a publication which contains the efforts of aspiring versifiers because Anne herself was a young poet whose work was very interesting indeed.

Valerie and I visited Richard Cole and his wife not so long ago and had a very happy morning together. Like his namesake, Old King Cole, Richard is a merry old soul – and always was. He knows that he has a huge number of friends on whom he can rely for support or help and we can assure him that for us it is a privilege to be his friends. He has a delightful family and home. It is very appropriate that this volume should be compiled as a tribute to his fortitude.

To all readers and writers I offer my very best wishes.

Ken Pearce

(Principal of MHGS 1973-1987)

June 2007

Section 1

The Baron

The Baron in the Shower

Judith Anderson (née Shaw)

In the shower Old Baron Cole
In all his glory to behol'
Girls he liked to tease,
Girls he'd wanted to please,
But his wife he had to cajole.....

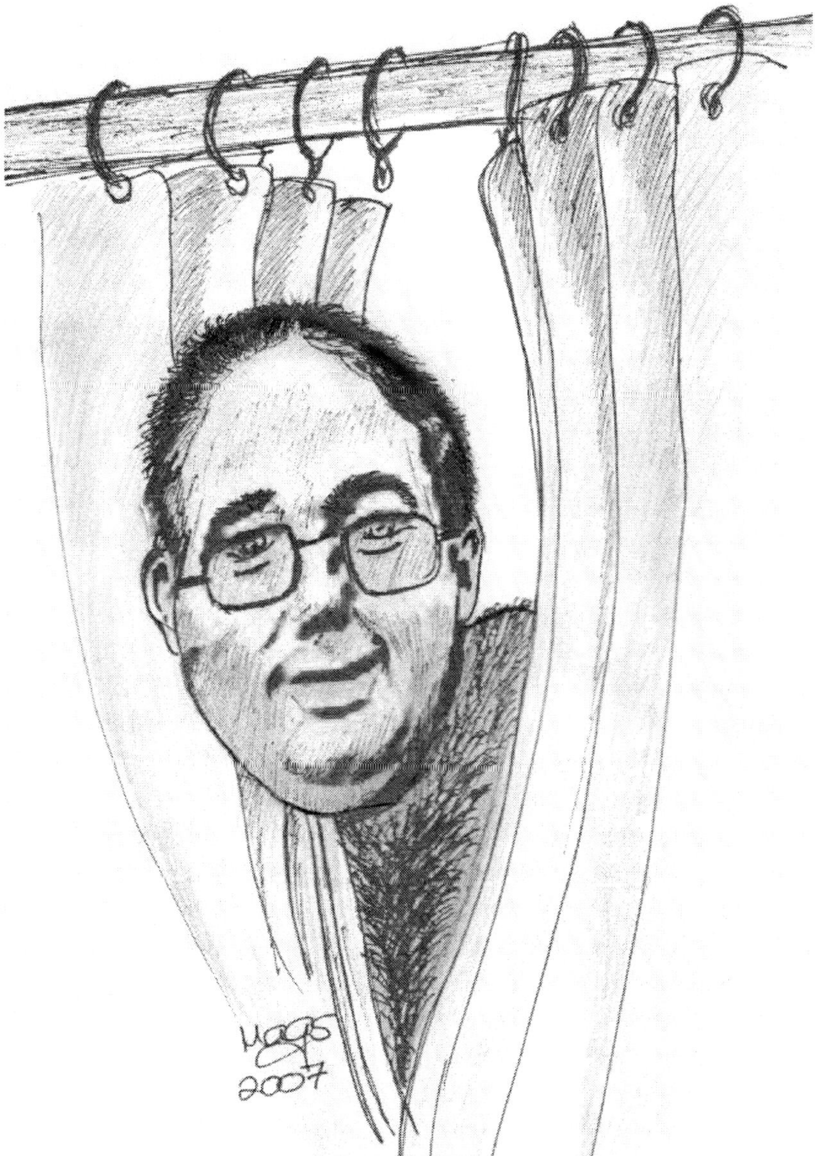
Mags
2007

The Baron's Trick

Gaynor Curry

There once was a 'Baron' called Rick
Who had a fabulous trick?
He'd rub soap on his bum,
Then skid on the scum
And we'd laugh until we were sick.

(Gaynor, Steve's wife)

The Magical Moving Chair

Alison Cookson (née Mayer)

Our Rich has installed upon his stair
An amazing magical moving chair.
The Coles should charge five,
If you want a ride -
It's better than a ride at the fair.

"Come Fly With Me..."

Ian Allchin

A fair young maiden named Jan Free
Decided she just had to flee,
She hitched a quick lift
On Baron's stair lift
But flew out and went up a tree!

The Boy Who Loved Swirls

Judith Anderson (née Shaw)

There was a fine young boy called Rick
Who was such an utter brick.
He loved the stylish girls
When they did all the swirls,
In reality they thought him a prick!

"What's in a Name?"

Alison Cookson (née Mayer)

Baron Ricardo Claude Von Floppenstappen,
Now how on earth did that name happen?
Well, when Kreb changed his name,
Rich said, "I'll do the same."
He never was one to be caught nappin'!

(Kreb Dragonrider had changed his name by deed poll from David Townsend and Richard Cole jokingly said he'd do the same!)

Special Agent

Liz Brown

Special agent, Madame Kittikat3941, is working with
the Ministry of Feline Interests for a reason,
On a secret mission, to capture the elusive culprit,
codenamed BW66, guilty of trespass and treason,
A sleek and slender princess, with prowess and magical
powers, she ensnares BW66 to his fate,
And obeying Baron Cole's instructions, with the help of
Gilbert the gull and his team mates,
Operation Seduction's plan is to drop the bugger into
Castle Cole's guano-filled moat this season.

(Andrew Bougeard aka BW66 and Ann Smith aka Kittikat)

Dodgy Tax Collector!

Liz Brown and Peter Mugridge

There was once a baron called Cole,
Whose work was as good as the dole?
Alas! He turned out to be a dodgy mole,
Overcharging clients' tax was his role.
Took up lap dancing round the pole,
Thus was pushed down a bloody great hole!

Broken Leg

Liz Brown

Here lies Richard, the invalid who broke his leg,
His right limb held in traction and hanging by a peg,
Cursing at the doctors, for deliberately delaying his op,
Now in Recovery Ward 17, drinking gallons of pop,
And flirting very happily with a staff nurse called Meg.

The Rambler's Blog

Judith Anderson (née Shaw)

A young man called Rick came across the bog
On his travels in the guise of Mr Fogg;
He called on Mr Fixit
To come and eat biscuit
And found it all written up in his blog.

Wedding Guests

Alison Cookson (née Mayer)

Coles are off to a wedding this Sat,
No new dress and definitely no hat;
You'll look oh so fine,
Do have a good time,
Looked forward since the invite dropped on t'mat!

The Cole's Diner

Liz Brown

Come let us see the new fab Cole's Diner,
Official Launch and ribbon cut finer
By the big man who came
For one last shot at fame
And get his name printed, was a shiner!

A 1950's American Style Food Bar
Red and black uniform is the theme, but no cars
Served in style with wine
Meat on a spit, we dined
And drinking coke a' cola pop from a large jar.

An Ode to Uncle Richard

Laura and Michael Stubbings

Although this evening is a "bit of a Mary Hare" do
We need to say a few words about you too.
Uncle Richard, you are full of mischief and fun
We think you'll agree when we are done.

You have alternative names for friends and family,
Although Laura's was invented by her cousin Vicky
When Laura was born Vicky was still very young
And her definition "LorLor" still rolls off your
tongue.

Since we've been around your eyesight has always
been poor.
Michael soon learnt to keep his toys off the floor.
Then for him along came problem number two
A dog called Robert who could also chew.

Your table manners are very bad
Making Mum and Aunty Jane quite mad;
"Mind the table" and "Donaldy Duck Quack Attack"
Usually means you end up getting a smack.

You are such a naughty, awful man
And Laura and Michael are your number one fans.
Laura already knew how to slurp
But you quickly taught her how to burp.

One time when Laura was playing the recorder
You were certainly quite out of order
Changing the words of "Happy Birthday Aunty Jane"
Meant Laura stopped playing with laughter pains.

When camping or caravanning you are a "miserable
outdoor git"
M.O.G. for short, for in the tent or awning you sit.
You dislike the hot sun, and certain insects make you
mad
But the wasp-shaking competition with Colin was the
best fun you had.

Life is never boring when you are around,
As we and many others have found.
But, Uncle Richard, this name is not right for you
As to us you are our "Uncle Dicky Poo!"

(Laura and Michael, Colin's children)

Our Dear Friend RN Cole

Ian Allchin

There was once an old soul named Cole
Who thought he saw a little mole.
He had a closer look,
And he checked in his book,
And found that he has got some coal!

To Richard Cole

Alison Cookson (née Mayer)

The girls of the 1971 year
To Richard Cole we raise a big cheer
We hold you in our heart
Yes, right from the start
Our own lord, our Baron, we love you dear!

The Life of Richard Norman Cole

Liz Brown

Mary and Norman had a baby boy,
Named *Richard Norman*, he, their pride and joy.
Had lots of black hair
Loved the rocking chair
And beautiful smiles, he wasn't coy!

At four, his first kiss at school was with Ann,
She was after all, his number one fan.
With his very good charms
Gave a peck on the arm.
But she broke his heart, refusing to hold hands.

Swiftly, he followed her to Mary Hare.
Other girls swooned, enchanted by his flair,
With good looks that could kill,
Showed off his sporting skills,
And voted team captain, oh how he cared!

Very popular loved flirting at the school gates.
Played a game of nipple tweaking with his best mate.
His memorable fame? Crashing through the glass doors
Of Dulverton Hall, left blood and gore on the floor!
Teachers saved his life and that was his lucky fate.

At eighteen, met a girl called Jane, on Dartmoor.
Stealing his heart, she had him completely floored.
Wasted no time in getting married
They rode off in a white carriage
Fleeing to Woking from Devon, oh that was sore!

Baby Jennifer came, followed by Victoria,
Oh did the Cole family rejoice with euphoria!
Then along came Binky, the cat,
Who refused to sleep on the mat!
And Robert, a lovely Labrador, with Gloria.

Now Richard is forty-something
Has a lot of experience to bring.
Two daughters growing in their teens.
And Jane, his loving wife, is keen
To bring home awareness of MND ring…

Section 2

School Life

Arlington Manor
Liz Brown

The Arlington Manor is a special place of scientific interest,
Bought in 1946, for a cool £22,000 was no jest!
Beautiful country mansion converted to a grammar school,
For bright deaf children to live and learn, play and obey the rules,
A special education encouraged them to do their very best.

Mary Adelaide Hare
Liz Brown

A lady in green called Miss Mary Adelaide Hare,
Set up a special school for deaf children in her care,
Oralist education was the mistress' plan,
Selecting bright children from up and down the land,
Her pupils thrived and graduated with skills to share.

Daffodils at Arlington Manor

Liz Brown

The meadow was flushed with daffodils,
Till some girl called Ali came with Gill.
Not to pull any punches,
They picked several bunches,
And scarpered off home for a vase to fill!

(Alison Cookson, (née Mayer) was convinced that pupils were allowed to take home a bunch of flowers for their parents but most of her friends don't even remember doing this!)

Mary Hare Days

Gillian Frazer (née Spence)

Remember that school, Mary Hare?
The days of mischief we had there?
All the games that we played,
All the jokes that we made,
And that green uniform they made us wear?

School Friends

Alison Cookson (née Mayer)

Many good things I take from my time at school,
Apart from learning which is norm'ly the rule.
But the ones which stand out
Without a shred of a doubt,
Are my buddies, my chums, my comrades - they're cool.

We have continued to meet, brother and sister,
We're companions; we're friends, familiar supporters.
We're each other's confidants,
Call us the agony aunts!
We're comrades through life; we're each other's well wisher.

There's nowt so important in this life as having good friends,
The girls of our year intake are such a nice blend.
Let's not forget the boys,
Full of noise and of ploys.
Together through this life we will wend.

(Friend: a person who has a strong liking for and trust in other really close friends who like to do everything together and are always sharing secrets [quoted from Merriam-Webster])

Summer Holidays

Laura Stubbings

They are the best holidays ever made.
Time to mess around and meet up with friends.
I hope and pray summer will never fade.
I cry when summer actually ends.

To parks and different places we go.
Everywhere we visit is great great fun.
It is so fab and I will tell you so.
Oh how I love the boiling hot lush sun.

The sun has power it makes me lazy.
When I'm out in the sun I get a tan.
The sun helps to grow the pretty daisies.
I always have a drink out of a can.

Out in the sun I have wonderful fun.
The thing I adore the most is the sun.

Speech Day

Liz Brown

Speech Day, a boring annual event.
It gave teachers the time to invent
Prizes for good speech,
For those who could reach,
The top of the competition air vent.

One was curious who the VIP would be?
And heaven forbid if one dared talk to me.
We met up in Dulverton Hall.
And hoped the curtain would fall,
So we could rush off for our cuppa tea.

We sat silently for speech we could not hear,
Oh where was the interpreter to give us the cheer?
All we got was waffle,
As the noise was muffled.
But reading the programme, helped to halt our fears.

Mums and Dads sat at the back
Whilst we kids sat on the rack.
Our rear end was sore,
From kneeling on the floor.
To win a prize, I wish I had the knack!

At last, all clapped and gathered round
For tea and cakes in the school ground,
Families hugged and kissed,
Sorry to have been missed
By school mates waiting for homeward bound.

Cross Country

Susan Slater

I feel nervous when I come out of the changing room,
The BANG! of the gun makes me feel more nervous,
And off we go!

I run through the muddy fields,
And up and down,
Turn left and right,
Across the road,
Into the woods where I get myself scratched.

I thought that my friends would be clapping for me,
Suddenly everything went out of my mind,
I found myself walking
So I began to run again.
Then I saw the winning post,
I came????

Sports Day

Liz Brown

Every year in sunny May,
Four house teams vie for Sports Day.
Arnold mostly came top,
Beverley was a flop!
Mary Hare and Braidwood frayed.

Field and track events, big news of the day
Followed by swimming in that grotty bay!
All teachers mucked in well,
Marshalled and rang the bell.
The principal was having a field day!

Selected runners stood at starting line,
Ready to flee to finishing tape line.
Huffing and hard panting,
To sweat and loud chanting,
From pupils and parents yelling so fine!

Pistol shot at start of relay race
House captains screaming loud and red faced!
Four ran round a large track
Batons at the ready…cracked!
Under the pressure of such fast pace!

Swimming was a natural flair,
Javelin thrown high in the air!
Discus went flying wide,
Shot putt crashed into side
Of cricket hut with undue care!

Out came the measuring stick
Synchronised stopwatches ticked.
Marshal cried "Disqualified!"
For some cheater who so tried
To get a medal for being a prick!

Tug-of-war with a long twisted rope
Tugging and pulling hard on the slope.
Long jumps stretched so far,
High jumps were on a par.
But oh boy! Did teacher have a mope!

Long-distance runner went the extra mile,
Doing 1500m took a long while.
100m was a quick sprint,
To get first place was pure mint.
The sports teacher was oh so stressed with piles!

Running so slow, down the outside lane
Jumping wobbly hurdles was a pain.
The three legged race was so funny!
The egg and spoon, oh not so crummy,
That sack race, a comical farce again!

At last, Sports Day came to another end.
Arnold cheered to get the trophies again!
Off to Blount Hall for tea and cakes,
Dulverton Hall for cup prize fakes.
Then home to family for long weekend!

"Only One Life..."

Alison Cookson (née Mayer)

In the year of 1971
When my life had hardly yet begun,
(I was only a child,
Had lived a wee while)
I took the 11^+ entrance exam.

I wanted to go to Mary Hare.
You see, my big brother had gone there,
He was in the Pig Club,
And I said that I would
Soon as I arrived, buy a share.

(Pupils could buy shares in the Pig Club. I did so, and when the club folded soon after my arrival, I made a profit on my shares!!)

I passed the exam, went for an interview,
Lesley looked after me - someone I knew.
I thought we were in BERK-shire
They said we were in BARK-shire!
But I enjoyed it and time it really flew.

In September I was in the first form
The first thing, I was shown to my dorm,
It was called Thomas Arnold.
Where later I learned to fold
Sheets - hospital corners being the norm.

My neighbour was a certain Janice Key
We had fun and in the dark of night we
Pretended to phone
Each other or home,
We had left our hearing aids on, you see.

We had lots of opportunities for sport
And places to play and to cavort,
A new swim pool
Was at our school –
As good as any holiday resort!

Fun to be had if good enough you were deemed
To play in the hockey, rounders or netball team.
Footballers and cricketers,
Athletes and swimmers,
Mary Hare was the happy sportsman's dream.

That year the master of all was Askew,
But he was to be replaced by someone new.
New headmaster Pearce
Was not a bit fierce,
Let himself in for, did he have a clue?

In the second year my dorm was Mundin
My dear friends became my new kith and kin.
We told our pal Van
Come when you can,
Ah ha - the fun was about to begin!

(Most of our 'gang' had been put together in this dorm, except for Vanessa who was most put out!)

My third year dormitory was Graham Bell;
This is a year that I remember well.
Van saw a she ghost,
Went white as a post,
Oh she thought that was the dorm from hell!

And from that time there's a story to tell
From the window Ali's teddy did fell;
Let's not beat 'bout the bush,
Our Teddy was pushed
And did our Ali play merry hell?!

And Ju asked Al how to spell battleship,
Late at night when we should all have kipped.
But our Ju slept-walked,
And our Ju slept-talked,
It's a small wonder our Ali didn't flip!

(We used to spend a lot of spare time playing battleships, Judith obviously dreamt about it too!)

In Eicholz I slept while in the 4th form,
We changed every year, this is the norm *
And the boys they did long
For wine, women and song.
But with studying - they had to conform.

*(*Changed dorms, that is - and the boys were of course growing up)*

When we were young ladies we stayed in Braidwood.
We were come to the end of our little girl-hood.
But there wasn't much food
As a general rule
And we had midnight feasts whenever we could!

In my final year I shared with a pal,
She was a good and hardworking young gal.
And so my ‘chum’ Liz
At math was a whiz
And on her way to being a Femme Fatale!

(Well, it rhymes!)

So here endeth my story, there’s no more to tell
Of life at Mary Hare with the clang of that bell,
Of cross country runs,
And sharp javelins.
So from me to you – it’s a cheery farewell.

Sunday Walks

Alison Cookson (née Mayer)

Every Sunday we went for a short walk,
We friends would wander and we would talk,
On Snelsmore and Greenham,
At Curridge and Crookham,
Saw wildlife but did not hear the birds squawk.

Another Life

Lesley Kiddell

1972 – We are all NEW!
Green knickers up to our arms,
Flat Clarke's brown shoes.
Hiding all our charms,
UGH!
We can't even choose.
Lots of tears,
Bed at half past seven,
We want our Mummy dears,
Home is definitely heaven.

1973 - It's impossible to be free,
Still finding out how everything works,
Homework not done – you wait and see.
GULP!
Behind each door a teacher lurks,
Discover boys, they are so cute,
Stolen kisses hand holding,
Get caught. Help! Boys get the boot
And girls get a jolly good scolding.

1974 - Enter the 3rd form door,
We adore Starsky and Hutch.
Squashed round the TV we want more,
Boys call them Car keys and clutch!
Fire alarms at night are so fun,
We get to see our darling boys.
Our sexy dressing gowns slightly undone,
One of our extra special joys.

1975 - feeling quite alive
Summer is fun, sun is out.
It's so hot, hot, hot,
School disco we twist and pout,
Mr. Fawkes has lost the plot.
Winter -decorate the hall,
For Christmas time.
Its great cos we all
Don't have to go to bed till nine.

1976 - still up to our tricks
Sweet sixteen.
Having our kicks,
Life is such a dream.
Revision time,
5am in the washroom,
Swotting Shakespeare rhyme,
And Macbeth's doom.

1977 - We are in heaven,
Queen's Silver Jubilee,
Star Wars comes out,
Wow, so much to see.
Waving union Jacks we all shout,
Then-Elvis Presley is DEAD!
Oh how sad,
Let's paint the coffee bar red,
And make an apple pie bed.

1978 – This year we hate,
Our last year as a gang.
Bye by friends, bye bye lovers,
The final school bell rang.
We go back to our Mothers,
School days are the best of our life.
Easy going so carefree,
Enter now a new world of strife,
We don't want this responsibility.

Together we were family,
Our lives, our loves our joys our sorrows.
Will always bind us together and we
Will continue to share each other's tomorrows.
No matter where we are,
Even in the whole world over
We have a bond so rare.
And it's called........
Mary Hare.

Once Upon a Time in Leafy Berkshire

Andrew Bougeard

Once upon a time in leafy Berkshire
A very naive and innocent young lad
Discovered girls galore in every size
Very soon that poor lad became bad.

The absolute shock of haircuts from hell,
The rantings of a man draped in black
Yes, hard times, yet some were so swell
Tales of the birds and bees a distinct lack.

Wildly our merry little gang did play football
In forbidden places where no ball should be,
Not a playground, but to some a hallowed hall
Were we lucky the gowned ones did not see.

Our Sundays could be fun, especially walks
Innocence lost on the common of Snelsmore.
So many girls, many miles and so many talks
No wonder night falls deep sleep and a snore.

So very, very strange that when children of our own
Come along we can somehow never tell the wicked tale,
Of the younger days wild and wicked we have known
Adventures that would have made our parents pale.

The years fly by getting older and perhaps wiser
Sometimes thinking to myself, "Was that really me?"
Perhaps realizing that school was merely an appetizer
For that big, wide, wicked world lying in wait outside.

Science Homework on Neutralisation

Laura Stubbings

I put a red mouse into the hat.
A piece of blue cheese was added to that.
I said the charm,
And shook my arm.
And I pulled out a fat green cat!

(Neutralisation: working on acid and alkaline)

Poxy Prefects!

Liz Brown

Prefects were nominated by staff,
Throwing their weight about was a laff!
Watched us study at prep time,
But we didn't give a dime.
They were no more than a load of flaff!

The Last Morning

Ann Smith

Early I rose that last June morning,
While all were a-slumber, I washed and dressed,
Went to the Covered Way, and let myself out,
To commune with memories of the past seven years.

The Summer House beckoned, and there I stole,
Those welcoming walls, so familiar and kind,
Soon to be out of bounds, through no punishment
 or misdeed,
But by the passage of time which leads to our departures.

I sat on the steps and looked down at the fields,
The mist was dissolving in the early morning sun,
The serenity and beauty were all that I needed
To feed the sadness lying heavy on my heart.

My memory recalled the happy times
And none could compare with friends and lovers.
How could I bear to say goodbye,
What would life be after Mary Hare?

The rest of the morning is now a blur,
The usual rush for tickets and trains.
Missing already those gone earlier
Everything unreal, it couldn't be true.

The clock of time has ticked now thirty years
And I have found goodbye is never said.
The Mary Hare family grows larger and larger
With new and old friendships, and fun times and
 laughter.

Section 3

The Teachers and Matrons

The Headmaster

Liz Brown

There was a Headmaster called Pearce,
Who came across as very fierce.
Nah, he was a softie,
Humorous and lofty,
A kindly soul, and quite sincere.

Deputy Head

Alison Cookson (née Mayer)

Our Deputy Head was Mr Bill Fawkes
Ever so strict and with eyes like a hawk
Encouraged us to sing,
Play a musical thing.
In any number of tongues he could talk.

(Mr Fawkes taught music, and had an amazing flair for languages)

The Ever-strict Mr Fawkes

Gillian Frazer (née Spence)

Our deputy Head, Mr Fawkes,
Said, "If anyone giggles or talks,
I'll send you to the Head,
And it'll be early to bed,
So don't interrupt me, you dorks!"

The Chemistry Teacher

Alison Cookson (née Mayer)

Chemistry was taught by Mr Ken Ward
Chemical Elements he wrote on t'board.
Boron and Hydrogen,
Neon and silicon,
Well, they all just had me utterly floored.

The Cookery Teacher

Alison Cookson (née Mayer)

Our nice cookery teacher Mrs Clews
Taught us all how to produce some good food.
About sponge and jam,
Sausage, eggs and ham,
Passed the O Level with grade A - great news!

The French Teacher

Alison Cookson (née Mayer)

French was taught by our Mr Keen, Peter,
On the subject my mind it would teeter.
Oh he would lament
About my accent,
He wished that I would speak a bit neater.

The Geography Teacher

Alison Cookson (née Mayer)

There was teacher who was full of fun,
His name was Mr Philip Ireson.
Taught Geography
Liked Photography
And you could rely on him for a pun.

The History Teachers

Liz Brown

Miss Roberts and Mrs Hill taught History.
We visited scenes of carnage and victory.
The naughty boys played jokes,
Dropped stink bombs that choked,
In the British museum, that's a true story!

(In my second year, we went on a school trip to London and there was a joke shop close by to the Museum. One of the boys asked for permission to visit the shops, and the rest is, well, history and we got a stern telling off by the Principal at the assembly next morning!)

The Maths Teacher

Liz Brown

If you look to the right,
You will see Mr Wright,
He taught Maths and games,
But boys got the blame,
For not being so bright!

The Needlework Teacher

Liz Brown

Mrs Ansell liked us to sew with some tack.
Apron and skirt making, confidence I lack.
She said, "A stitch in time saves nine" -
This subject is no fad of mine,
I scored nine in an exam and thus got the sack!

(In my second year, I failed the Christmas exam scoring a very low nine percent, and my family teased me saying it because I only knew how to thread a needle!)

Mr Music Man

Liz Brown

Old Bill Fawkes was an enthusiastic music man,
He encouraged us to be an orchestra clan.
Playing instruments was a boon
Who cared if we were out of tune?
If you could play one musical note, you were a fan!

Our Bill would tap his fingers on the piano,
Two guitarists standing between him, sung at high alto;
A little lad banging at the drums,
Flutes not quite in harmony, oh crumbs!
Ah! What joy it was to make such noises having a go.

Mr Kell's Dog

Gillian Frazer (née Spence)

Mr Kell had a dog named Seamus,
An Alsatian he was and quite famous,
He'd run after a ball,
Both big ones and small,
We loved him and, you know, can you blame us?

SEAMUS
Mags
2007

A Song for Matron

Lesley Kiddell

Chorus:

O Mary Hare,
Oh rain rolling in from
Snelsmore Common, my desire,
Is always to be here,
O Mary Hare.

1. Too much do we work 'cos the teachers are mean.
A mixed pot we are in uniforms of green.
Past the sick bay, gosh, the Chemistry lab's on fire.
Chasing the first formers is Miss MacIntyre.

Chorus

2. Sweep through the hall, hey girls, look at those men
Oh please, carry us back to the days we knew then,
Christmas time singing, we a heavenly choir,
Joined by staff, Mr Fawkes and, of course,
Miss MacIntyre.

Chorus

3. Smiles in summer house and tears on the train,
Because we have to go home yet again.
Mary Hare is our heart's desire.
And, of course, let's remember dear
Miss MacIntyre.

Chorus

(Lesley says: "Apologies to "Mull of Kintyre." I did this when I was about 17 or 18 in 1978 as a tribute to Miss MacIntyre who was the nicest Matron.")

My Friend, the Matron

Barry Avison

Sleeping in bed snoring away
The sun is up for another day.
There I am, dreaming of girls,
And being the best bloke in the world.
I'm nice and warm, its cold outside,
The rising sun shines in my eyes.

Thump! Thump! Here she comes
"It's seven o'clock, come on get up!"

Thump! Thump! Here she comes
"It's half-past seven, come on get up!"

Who on earth pulled my blanket over?
Oh, it must be her, who else could it be.
I bring it back before I freeze.
Ah, its nice and warm once again.
I wish that matron would be my friend,
This was the best sleep I've had,
Why should it end so bad?

Thump! Thump! Here she comes
"Your breakfast's cold, come on get up!

Groan, I get up .....

The Nagging Matron

Liz Brown

We had a matron called Miss Knagg.
She looked like a really old hag.
She picked on the young boys,
Would not let them have joy,
And moaned if anyone had a fag!

Goodnight from Matron

Gillian Frazer (née Spence)

Miss Annabel and Miss Morey
Would never read a bedtime story,
They'd say, "Goodnight,"
And turn out the light,
And if we played up, they'd floor ye.

Section 4

School Friends

Double Trouble

Liz Brown

Two little boys met on a train
Rich and Jon, oh they're so vain!
Mischief was their big game,
To enter Big Hall of Fame
Alas! They were a double pain!

Form 1A 1971

Gillian Frazer (née Spence)

Jonathan Farthing was fair-haired and tall,
Andrew Turner was brown-haired and small,
David Walker was vocal,
Stephen Saunders lived local,
But the girls were the smartest of them all.

Experiences of a First Former

Judith Anderson (née Shaw)

There was a young lady named Vanessa,
Whose teachers tended to depress her;
So away she went,
Down to the basement,
And found a nice young man to impress her.
(Vanessa Barrow)

There was a young girl called Jane
Who rolled around in such pain;
The doctor was called
And was appalled,
Her midnight feasts had been in vain!
(Jane Robinson)

There was a young girl called Kath
Who found herself down the wrong path;
She ventured to the Common
And came across a white swan,
And didn't come home for her weekly bath!
(Katharine Burrow)

There was a young boy called Ian, from Kent,
Who didn't know if he came or went?
He chased the girls
And gave them swirls,
And now his legs are permanently bent!
(Ian Allchin)

Form 4H

Louise McKenzie

Matty, the ginger-haired boy,
Who draws and draws;
Timmy, the tall, tall boy,
Who reads and reads;
Rupert, the woody bear,
Who fights and fights;
Gail, the blue-eyed girl,
Who dreams and dreams;
Karen, the sleepy-head girl,
Who sleeps and sleeps;
Fiona, the telly-mad girl,
Who watches and watches;
Terry, the cracker boy,
Who talks and talks;
Paul, the Irish boy,
Who plays and plays,
Are the people in my form!

An Avid Train Spotter

Liz Brown

A young man from Epsom had a wild fetish for trains,
Muggy is the name, tells of car journeys being a pain.
"Economical by rail," he cried aloud,
"Avoid speed cameras by zipping through the clouds!"
Weary and worn while spotting, he collapsed from the
strain.

(Peter Mugridge aka Muggy is a very enthusiastic train traveller)

The Sleepwalker

Gillian Frazer (née Spence)

Judith Anne Shaw used to sleepwalk at night,
If we were up and saw her, she'd give us a fright.
She'd catch you alone,
Saying in a monotone,
"How do you spell battleships?" Yes, that's right!

How do you spell battleships?
Mags 2007

The Crushes of Alison

Gillian Frazer (née Spence)

Now Ali fancied most of the male staff!
This gentle failing did make me laugh.
Each evening she'd ponder
Some teacher out yonder,
While I'd just say, "Not him, he's naff!"

Brown Eyes? Blind Eyes More Like!

Ian Allchin

Young Liz Brown is going on the prowl,
With her eyes wide open like an owl.
She espy a lad,
And isn't she glad
That the nice gorilla didn't growl!

Judith's Young Man

Gillian Frazer (née Spence)

Judith had a young man called Jerry
Who was fond of a glass of sherry,
He drank seven glasses,
And ogled all the lasses.
Was our Judith angry? Very!

Little Ju

Ian Allchin

There was a young lass named Judith Shaw
Who liked to have a cold drink with straw,
But her man Jerry
Was a bit merry
And mistook her for Ali McGraw!

The Way to a Mans' Heart

Alison Cookson (née Mayer)

There was a fine handsome man called Stu,
Who decided it was time to woo.
He called upon Fran,
Said, "Get my bran!"
Now she gets his breakfast, bread, butter and stew.

Big Jon

Ian Allchin

A young chap named Jon Brown,
Is known for his big frown.
He met a gal
Whose name is Sal,
And now we have more Browns.

("Groan!" I hear you say)

Amazing Swimmer Judith McCready

Gillian Frazer (née Spence)

Swimmer Judith McCready could do butterfly,
So impressive we all shouted "My! My!"
She'd glide through the pool,
So stunning and cool,
That all we could do was gape and stand by.

My Best Friends

Liz Brown

My best friends were Sharon and Helen.
We played a game of throwing melons.
Shooting practice at netball
Till one of us had a big fall,
And that was the end of our Helen!

The Cleveland Way Challenge

Janet Wardle, Barbara Brown, Mags Adams,
Helen Shirley, Mike Aston and Martin Broomfield

We, six intrepid walkers, from all corners of the land
Rose to meet the Cleveland Way Challenge.

\- One hundred and nine miles -
Persistent Mike soldiered us six on.

Over hill, over moor
Through hail, through rain.

With miles of smiles
We weathered on through
wind and sunshine.

Our leader's soft spot was blackberries
Which hung on brambles
like forbidden fruit.

Dozy Martin with his drooping eyes
Ate the miles away with
doughnuts and pies.

Limping Mags, stoically bearing
upwards and onwards, Tripped the
miles away with her flashy shorts.

Chatty Barbara talked the miles away.
And soothed aching feet
much to our delight.

Blistery Helen muddled and
laughed the miles away, Her
hands were glued to the first aid box.

Starstruck Janet romanced the miles away
With dreams of her new-found love.

With Helmsley one hundred and
nine miles behind us. Our goal
Filey, was a welcome sight!

Proposed Walk – June 2007

Alison Cookson (née Mayer)

There were three ladies, Ali, Ju and Gill
Who decided they would stride down glen and up hill.
Let's do th' West Highland Way
We'll do it, come what may
Sun, rain or hail, we'll do it, we will.

Three Hiked the West Highland Way

Alison Cookson (née Mayer)

We three friends went off on a holiday
Right after the very end of May
Ali, Ju and Gill
They climbed every hill,
Walked every path of the West Highland Way.

Visit by a Muse

Alison Cookson (née Mayer)

One night when away our Ju could not sleep
Her thoughts were running too wide and too deep,
So she sat on the floor
Out in the corridor
Limericks she composed, read 'em and weep.

Gill Aims High

Alison Cookson (née Mayer)

"We'll climb Everest," said Gill to our Daisy.
"No", said Daisy, it's totally crazy."
Gill said, "Don't be idle,
Up that hill we'll sidle.
Get off your backside and don't be so lazy!"

(Alison Cookson aka Daisy)

A Roll in the Heather

Jerry Anderson

Three ladies one day
On the West Highland Way.
Were waiting for a break in the weather.
They met a young man,
With a gorgeous brown tan.
So they rolled him around in the heather... *(I wish!!)*

(Jerry, Judith's husband)

The West Highland Way

Judith Anderson (née Shaw)

Three young ladies set off on their walk.
Loved the paths when able to talk,
Jostled from side to side,
When the path was not wide,
Until one of them decided to squawk...

(With a bit of inspiration from Ali and Gill)

Birds of a Feather

Alison Cookson (née Mayer)

Ali, Judi and Gill got together
On MSN, these birds of a feather.
They tried their very best,
But got into a mess,
And instead of composing would blether…

Gill of Red Bee Media

Ian Allchin

A lass working for Red Bee Media
Has just had a very great idea.
To be an audiologist,
She got the very basic gist,
Not to use her encyclopaedia.

Inmates' Drinking Holiday! - August 2006

Alison Cookson (née Mayer)

Fifteen inmates from the '71 year
Said let's go on holiday, drink some beer,
They visited Skipton,
Played rounders and whipped 'em
And climbed rocks at Brimham which was just near.

Scarborough Holiday 2007

Alison Cookson (née Mayer)

From Mary Hare thirteen of us cried "Woh!
Let's all to Yorkshire on holiday go."
Site was down farm track,
Three miles there and back,
We stayed on a quiet camp site you know.

The Baron and Baroness bring Sunshine

Alison Cookson (née Mayer)

Rick came along too, chauffeured by Jane,
Who drove each motorway, each country lane.
She brought his good chair
So he would sit there,
They brought us warm sunshine and no rain!!!!

Cadac Curry Chef

Judith Anderson (née Shaw)

Gill's Cadac Curry Chef cooks well.
"Oh!" they all said, "that's swell"
Said Ali, "Oh gosh!
That seems dead posh."
And it gave off a beautiful smell...

To Catch a Fish for Tea

Tom Anderson

A dozen of us left the quay
To try and catch something for tea.
We didn't fish well,
Because of the swell
And Jazzeh was sick in the sea.

I've Caught Me a Cod!

Rachel and Judith Anderson (née Shaw)

We improved as time went on
The sun came out and shone.
Ju said, "My God!
I've caught me a cod!"
But golly it didn't half pong...

Crazy Burner!

Rachel and Tom Anderson

Janc Cole and Doreen got a fright:
Their crazy burner caught alight!
All crowded around
And shrieked at the ground
Doreen blew (in vain, with hindsight).

(Rachel and Tom, Judith's children)

Colin to the Rescue!

Rachel and Tom Anderson

Everyone started to yowl
But, with his Patronus (an owl),
Colin stepped in,
With boots made of tin
And smothered the blaze with a towel!

Richard's Our Witness

Judith Anderson (née Shaw)

Richard in his wide-brimmed hat
Watched us all use a rounders bat.
Liz V was drunk,
Georgie got a thunk,
We lost the match, and that was that!

Rivalry

Vanessa Gee (née Barrow) and Frances Ewing

A pupil called Van
Became friends with Fran,
They passed on notes
To have a vote
Who would get their man?

My First Love

Liz Brown

My first love was a boy called Harry.
He, the guy, I thought I'd marry.
In the Love House, we kissed,
But got caught by the Miss.
Our sins to bear, we had to carry.

Section 5

The Mary Hare History Forumites

Mary Hare History Forum

Alison Cookson (née Mayer)

We all used to meet up on Yahoo
But there was some kind of "to do",
Kreb set up this forum,
Kept us from boredom,
Now numbers are up to one eight-two.

(Numbers of members of the forum continue to grow steadily)

Mary Hare History Forum Webmaster

Liz Brown

There was an old man called Kreb,
Who loves to sit and surf the web,
He monitors posts and awards points,
To those who dare rub his creaky joints,
Thus, he finally hooked up with a beaut called Deb.

Limerick Competition

Alison Cookson (née Mayer)

There is a webmaster called Kreb,
Who asked us way back in Feb ,
For the best limerick.
Will it be Tim or Rick?
Won't be me, I'm orff, back t'me shed!

Limerick Contests

Liz Brown

Limerick contests are fun and easy do,
One can think laterally whilst sitting on the loo,
Competition is rife,
But nitpickers are strife,
To rid of those pedants, let put them in the zoo!

(There were a few forumites who tended to 'nit pick' other forumites' posts, hence the name 'pedants' arose and the Nitpick Inner Circle was formed)

A Three-way Tie

Alison Cookson (née Mayer)

In our limerick contest three have tied
Although several others did but try,
To the form pedants
Brown Eyes says "Pants"
Syllables she uses many- is she fried?

(I wrote this after three of us had won the same number of votes after the first round of voting in the limerick contest, including Liz Brown (aka Brown Eyes) who was still not quite sticking to the usual limerick format)

A Bee in a Bonnet

Alison Cookson (née Mayer)

There was a fine young lady called Janfree
Who into her bonnet got a bee.
"For Brown Eyes I'll vote,
Whatever she wrote,
And whatever will be will be!"

(Janet Freestone a keen supporter of deaf poets, pointing out that the deaf are at a disadvantage when using English, and declared that the structure of the limerick was unimportant)

Ian Gets His Comeuppance

Ian Allchin

That Tea Boy is sure one cheeky man,
Though his limericks are a bit wan.
He lost to his pally
In a match with Ali.
And he's no more that cheeky bad man.

Sore Loser

Liz Brown

An infant boy called Ian Allchin-Ham,
Cried and spat his dummy out of the pram.
His limerick was a flop!
Stormed off in a major strop,
And humbly made BE some bread and jam.

(BE is short for Brown Eyes. Ham was added to make a double-barrelled name to rhyme!)

Peacemaker

Liz Brown

Ok, folks; let us call a truce,
Ian did try hard to seduce,
Now time for love and hugs,
To stop those lurking bugs,
Before forumites turn to puce!

"A Touch of Bubbly"

Alison Cookson (née Mayer)

Brown Eyes is our resident poet,
She's second to none, we all know it,
But limericks set form
Are totally reborn,
When our Liz has been at the Moet!

In a Tizz!

Alison Cookson (née Mayer)

There was a young lady called Gizmo
Oh, did she get in a big tizz-mo?
Used petrol at the pump
gave her 'Brummie' the hump
and caused her Mike to say more than, "Oh!"

(Mags Adams-Aston aka Gizmo ran out of petrol and it cost a pretty penny to get the car repaired. The car is known as 'Brummie')

Awaits with Bated Breath

Alison Cookson (née Mayer)

I look forward in anticipation
To see what our Peter has done.
Whatever he wrote,
there is no vote,
but come on and write, it's so much fun.

(On hearing that Peter Mugridge was intending to write some more limericks for the forum)

Cheeky!

Alison Cookson (née Mayer)

There was a young tike called Braidwood
Who asked Kittikat if she would
Dance nude on the' telly.
"Not on your nelly!"
Cried the pussycat from Boreham Wood!

(Andrew Bougeard aka Braidwood, Kittikat comes from Borehamwood)

Oh Daisy, what a Tease!

Andrew Bougeard

A dizzy blonde called Daisy
Had moments of being crazy,
Always taunting poor innocent Braidwood,
Who kept quiet, as a gentleman should,
But one day he won't be so lazy!

Mr Mischief

Liz Brown

BW-66 is a man of great mischief!
Loves to stir up trouble and cause our felines some grief,
Old Ginge and Le Chat Noir are of course no match,
For Princess Newbyrose and Kittikat can latch
Onto the seagull's foe and his freedom will be brief!

(Old Ginge and Le Chat Noir are mock adversaries of Newbyrose and Kittikat. All are feline characters. Le Chat Noir is a black cat, Old Ginge is an old ginger cat, and Newbyrose, a white cat, is an anagram for Brown Eyes)

Come to the Ball

Alison Cookson (née Mayer)

Do you hear our Peter Mugridge call,
"Oh, come to the forumite ball.
It's held in Cheshire,
There's nowhere better,
Oh come, you forumites, come one and all."

The Real McCoy

Alison Cookson (née Mayer)

There once was a young lad called Teaboy,
Who with our young lasses was not coy.
Yes, he's know to have been
With no less than 17,
Oh man, he thinks he's the real McCoy!

(Ian Allchin (aka Teaboy) of the 1971 intake had many girlfriends during his time at MH)

Sponsored Swim

Liz Brown

An old man named Ian, aka Teaboy now Twangboy,
Boasted conquests of taking 17 gals as his pride and joy,
Ali (his no.1), Gilly, Fiona, Ruth A, and Jane, to name
just a few,
Notched up an 88 lengths sponsored swim, recently in
the news,
To prove he has the knack, "Lucozade" and spinach was
his secret ploy!

(Ian swam 88 lengths to raise funds for MNDA and MHF)

Aloe Vera Sales Rep

Peter Mugridge

There once was a lady called Liz,
Who thought that AV was the biz;
She set up a stall,
To sell us them all,
And then she dissolved with a fizz.

Broken Romance

Liz Brown

A young lady by the name of Brown Eyes,
Found it difficult to say her goodbyes;
Walked out of the door, no looking back,
Heart torn in two, carrying a rucksack,
Romance with Rob over, he told her lies.

The Eyes Have It

Ian Allchin

Another young lady named Brown Eyes
Had her eyes on some very nice guys.
She decided to flirt,
But she forgot her skirt,
And now these guys got very wide eyes!

Back to School

Alison Cookson (née Mayer)

Our Muckyknees name is Gi~an,
On topics banal he likes a ban.
"I beg you to care,
Stick to Mary Hare."
Dare I mention any other? Yes, I can!

(Gian stated that he would prefer forumites to stick to talking about MH)

HRH Elaine

Liz Brown

Our Elaine has a secret to tell:
Her family tree is good news to sell.
A hint of royal blue blood,
Brought paparazzi in flood.
Nicknamed HRH, so bow or curtsy well!

HRH loves to watch TV soaps news.
Another interest: cooking home stews.
A famous author of books,
Elegant and charming looks,
Her posts, is a joy to read in the pews.

Aunty Elaine

Alison Cookson (née Mayer)

This forum is full of friends,
Old pals who want to make amends
And Sweet Aunt Elaine
Who's pretty, not plain
Keeps us all from going round the bend.

(Elaine, nicked-named 'Aunty' by Richard Cole, casts a sensible, calming influence on the forum)

Dizzy Blonde

Liz Brown

A dizzy blonde called Ali has just been given her own
special thread,

Proud to be a farmer's wife and daughter, that's her
butter and bread,

Loves to milk the cows and fills her huge bum-bag with
dairy,

Alas! She doesn't half realise, senility has made her into
a fairy,

Thus, the Nitpick Inner Circle are worried and filled
with dread!

(Alison Cookson (née Mayer) was delighted to be given her own special thread after a lot of teasing about blonde jokes)

Care Bears

Liz Brown

An arctophile named Janet, aka Teddygirl, started a
new thread on bears.

Such candour and artistic talent, the passion for
collecting teddies is her flair,

Took by storm, the sell-out of Mary Hare bears stock,
raising funds in the name of charity,

Theodore, Baron, Claude, Floppenstappen, Raymond
and Roosevelt, unusual names such a rarity,

So popular was the gathering of names, a virtual
teddy bear picnic was organised with efficient care!

Nagging

Vanessa Gee (née Barrow)

A young girl called BE,
Kept pestering Veegee.
Give me a poem,
With some decorum.
Then you can go for tea.

(Vanessa Barrow aka Veegee)

Answering the Call for More Poetry

Alison Cookson (née Mayer)

Have heard our Liz is tearing her hair out,
She's crying, raging and starting to shout!
She visited Ju,
Said "what a to do,
I want some more poems, limericks…. owt!"

Surprise Visitor!

Alison Cookson (née Mayer)

Judith got a visit from Brown Eyes
Who said, "O Judi, you're so wise
I'm in such a fix,
I need more limericks
Cos my book is a bit on the small size..."

Sherry Time

Alison Cookson (née Mayer)

One day Ju had a visitor called Liz
Unexpected so she got in a tizz.
They opened the sherry,
And got very merry.
Then Liz got her limericks done in a whizz.

Banter Between Two Friends on MSN

Alison Cookson (née Mayer) and Gillian Frazer (née Spence)

Gosh, Daisy, you have found your vocation,
Fairly raising your status and station.
Your limericks are rife,
About all walks of life,
And could be the best in the nation.

Oh Gilly you have chosen to speak
For this I waited week upon week
Your rhyme is catchy
Wicked and snatchy
Mine by comparison seem weak

Now Gilly a limerick can write
With humour and vigour and sprite;
Write one two or four,
Or even some more,
Then post them night upon night upon night.

Yes Gilly a limerick can pen
I guess you'd be able to write ten.
Put pen to paper,
And post it later,
Then write some more when back in your den.

Yesterday you wrote about Jo
But I can't remember how it did go
You mentioned a fell
And maybe a dell
But the exact words I really don't know.

So post your good limericks in here,
Others will raise an almighty cheer
To see Daisy matched,
Oh, or even thrashed
Winning the contest went to her head dear.

Now, Ali, I expected one reply not five
You've been as busy as a bee in a hive;
Limericks galore,
Witticisms and more,
You sure are keeping this contest alive!

Well Gilly this is my reply,
I'm not about to eat humble pie;
I know I'm the best
You put me to the test.
Cos in this comp there ain't no tie.

(With apologies to Gill, she knows why. Gill actually wrote this verse on my behalf during an earlier chat on MSN)

Bell Ringing

Liz Brown

A chap called Terry loves to ring his bells,
He ran up the belfry tower but fell,
Flew mid-air, grabbing the ropes,
Swinging like mad, prayed for hope,
Then slid to the bottom and lived to tell.

Mischievous Lot!

Liz Brown

Have you seen that mischievous lot?
Only the elite can join their pot.
Banned from twice-weekly chat room
For non '71 status, doom!
Pity, how do I get rid of that spot?

The Twelve Days of Christmas

Mags Adams-Aston, Ian Allchin, Andrew Bougeard,
Liz Brown, Kreb Dragonrider (David Townsend),
Sally Gallimore (née Ramsden), Martin Williams

On the Twelfth Day of Christmas, my forumites gave to me:

Twelve Krebs moderating
Eleven Stevies lolling
Ten Tipsy TeaBoys
Nine Frisky Felines
Eight Daisys Milking
Seven screaming Seagulls
Six Rameses
Five Gizmos
Four Nilpickers
Three French Spies
Two Brown Eyes
And a Baron in the Castle!

Section 6

All Creatures Great and Small

The Fox

Christine Powell

The fox with his beautiful tail
Shot over the green,
Then out popped his head
To see if there is a hunter seen.

The squirrels up in the trees
Chat and hop to one another,
Say to the fox,
"No, there isn't a hunter, dear brother."

On he goes, on the peaceful green
Full of scent of flowers.
The dew silently creeps away
When the flowers have their showers.

The fox with his beautiful tail
Runs from the hounds,
His feet swiftly gallop to his den
Down in the ground.

Nags
2007

The Bassett Hound

Zoe Churms

Those soulful eyes,
That large black nose,
Those droopy ears and awkward toes.

The leap so short,
Knobbly and stout,
That large wet tongue,
In a grinning mouth.

That nice smart suit,
Of white, black and brown,
And a long wavy tail,
The best in town.

A funny dog the Bassett is,
Though he loves to play and please,
His heart so warm with love for you,
No other dog can fill the gap he leaves.

"They're Off!"

Kathryn Prescott

The horses canter down to the start,
All the colours under the sun,
Bay, black, brown, grey, chestnut, dun.
The jockeys with their gay shirts,
Their horses' coats shine with health.
They all wait, tense,
The stalls open, they spring out,
Immediately the crowd cheer and shout
For their favourite horse.
A grey takes the lead,
The shouts become more frenzied.
As the horses flash by
The crowd is left behind.
The horses settle down,
A bay overtakes the grey.
A black overtakes the grey, and so it goes on
Until the last furlong.
Now every horse for himself,
The atmosphere is electric,
The horses strain against the jockeys' whips.
The roar of the crowd is past imagining.
"What price the Happy Hooker?"
"What price Pascualete?"
Goes up the cry,
As well as, "Come on, come on."
Everyone flashes past the post,
But a chestnut, with his neck
Stubbornly outstretched has won!

Beauty and the Beast

Liz Brown

A female cow called Daisy resides in a cattle shed,
Every morning she comes out to graze, until she well fed,
Chewing at the cud, squishing her tail at the flies,
Listening to gossip from her female bovine spies,
Then a scintillating stroll towards a bullock named Fred.

Scarborough Fair

Liz Brown

Our Daisy's off to Scarborough Fair
Holiday sunbathing, in deck chair.
Leaving behind, her bovine spies,
Sneaking off under plain disguise,
As farmer's pillion, the wind in her hair!

A Dog's Life

Helen Lamond

His soft brown eyes shine up at you,
Pleading for a bone to chew.
"A walk, a walk," his whimpers say,
His master's reply is, "Not today."

The next-door cat is great to chase,
But he knows if he does he'll be in disgrace.
Chased with a broom when caught in the larder,
Honestly, life couldn't be harder!

But curled up by his master at the end of the day
I'm sure most dogs could safely say,
"Although life's hard and not always fun,
There would be a long way to go for a better one!"

The Bird

Susan Gill

You are free,
Free to fly through the air
And land wherever you will.
Free, to come and go as you desire,
I envy your freedom,
Freedom from the pettiness of humanity.

The Carthorse's Lament

Zoe Churms

As the day the new day is dawning
And you hear the cock crow.
And you rise bright and early
To view the countryside below
You can see a shadowy figure.
In the shade of a tree
And you can hear a voice sighing.
As weary as can be.

I'm only an old carthorse
Living on trodden-down grass.
Skinny, ugly and bony
Thinking of days, long gone past
Of young days by my mother's side
Happy and carefree.
Bounding wild in the long grass
The whole world belonged to me.

Then a strange man came and put me in shafts
Along cobbled roads I would roam.
Delivering things, to oh so many firms
Till my master would ride me home.
Oh, how my back and legs ached
And the whip lash stings my sides.
And the rain soaked through my matted coat
While over the cobbles my feet slip and slide.

My back is raw and breaking
I'm broken-kneed and lame.
I can't pull now with the rest of the draft
And my spirit is like a dying flame.
The beautiful morning I no longer see
And my hearing is getting dim.
Remember, my friends, wherever you be
That man is the master and we just cannot win.

I'm only an old carthorse.
I'm old, lonely and grey.
My life is slowly ebbing out
And soon I'll be going away.
I graze in the meadow and swish my tail
And shake my head and neigh.
And I sing this song as my heart is breaking
I'll be going to the knackers today.

Dream Stallion

Mags Adams

As my head touched the pillow,
I fell into a dream of an Albino stallion
With flowing mane and tail,
Carrying grace, he held his head proudly,
Handsomely leading a herd of beautiful mares.
His hooves hardly touched the surface,
Eyes glittering like rubies,
Suddenly all heads drop down
To graze in peace.
The Albino stallion looked over the herd,
His head proudly in the air,
Mane flying in the wind, nostrils flared,
He gazed in pride at his mares.

Albino
Mags 2007

Section 7

Reflections

Beyond the Silence – Experiences before and after a Cochlear Implant

Suzie Maine (née Williams)

IMAGINE
Can you see my silent world?
Objects, people moving all around
Yet they make not one sound.

PEACEFUL
Seeing branches bending in the wind
Watching rainbows in my sleep
Impenetrable silence, so profound and deep.

LONELY
My bubble is complete
Look at me, I can see you
I am here in your world too.

FRUSTRATION
I try and try to get it right,
Moving lips that read so hard
Inches become an impossible yard.

JEALOUSY
I wish I could hear like you
Thrumming music all in my mind
It's not enough that you are kind.

EUPHORIA
Can that feeling be a sound I hear?
This is amazing quite a shock
My thoughts on life are in the dock.

CONFUSION
I do not know which way to turn
Is it loud to you in your ears?
Or quiet and gentle like my tears?

INTRUSION
I do not like this at all
I cannot let these sounds in easily
I feel mixed up, disorientated and queasy.

REALISATION
This new world is noisy!
I have to work to make it click
Just listening will do the trick!

DELIGHT
It is coming now
It is time to let them in
My old silence is in the bin!

REVERBERATION
A knocking on the outside door
A low-pitched, constant sound
Rather common, booming all around.

RHYTHMIC
An attention-grabbing mix of pitch
I like this noise, it is quite exciting
But rather hard to put in writing.

SIBILATION
I should be looking out for this!
A siren's warning emission
A quarrelling child's articulation.

WHISTLE
Something blowing over my microphone,
How like the gentle breezes blow
Quite melodic, nice and slow.

MUSICAL
You should try and resolve this first,
Can I really give a notion?
It is meant to be the ultimate emotion!

Wonderful, Dangerous World

Barry Avison

The future lies in Man's mind.
Knowing that the best or worst could come,
I wonder what it might be like,
In one hundred years' time.
Imagine ourselves going home
Not by bus, train, cars or bikes,
But by invisible transport
That will carry us from a place within seconds.
Pollution will be gone, because there will be no cars.
A wealth of luxuries can be bought.
Expensive? But they help to fill our empty lives.
What about the jobless, strikes and the dole?
A new kind of government, perhaps Communist,
Which is tearing the countryside,
Building machinery and digging holes,
For the last bit of oil to be turned into mist,
Into the air, into our lungs, and then we die.

Future Fashion

Helen Keightley

Gone the days of colourful fashion,
And out comes a shimmering world
Of stars, silver and glittering gold.
Gone the piles of unironed washing.
For every night a fresh garment appears
From the clothes-making machine.
The girls' eyelashes flutter with silver stardust,
And gold lipstick is a must!
The wigs are of stainless steel,
All shimmering with curls.
Rings and bangles flash with gold,
And nobody seems to grow old,
With all those beauty salons -
Oh lucky, lucky things!

Mags
2007

Spring

Rachel Peacock

Young Spring, dancing gaily,
And changing everything
From white to green,
Her hair flowing behind, the colour of gold.

Decked with flowers,
She throws them about,
Amid musical cheers from the birds,
Singing merrily and sweetly.

Bouncing along, so unlike Old Winter,
Her hair trailing,
She puts life on every flower and plant,
Her gay steps put Old Winter to shame.

Every living thing wakes up,
The stream flows gently,
The ice melts, all traces of Old Winter removed,
Spring is welcomed with joy.

Fresh green leaves come out,
Trees, no longer bare and unclothed,
And daisies adorn the green lawn,
The fountain comes to life again.

Once more the people have picnics,
As they watch Spring's work,
Coming to life,
Shown by the flowers peeping out of the ground.

A Hot Sunny Day in Summer

Susan Slater

A hot sunny day in summer,
Sun shining hot onto the pond,
Pond glittering and reflection.

Dragonflies flying around the pond,
Fishes swimming to a cool place.
Horses loiter about,
Wasps and bees buzzing around.

Lawn mower very noisy.
A crimson rose opening softly,
That puff smell of rose
Summer pools of fresh country air.

A Walk in a Forest

Mark Miller

One day I went crunch, crunch through the autumn leaves
As a gentle breeze came by,
Making all the old red-browny leaves fall,
As they fell, they floated as if they were sinking
Crunch, crunch went my feet.
A squirrel hopped and got an acorn,
Then it hopped to its tree.
Suddenly I saw a meandering stream....
Ssssh went the water.
Little flies crawled on the thin water top
Clip-clop went a horse going, buzzing flies swarming round its head.
As I walked by the rays of the sun, worth rough the Branches,
A deer peeping to see what the crunch, crunch was.
He saw me.
At the end of my walk crunching the leaves,
I hopped in the car and went home.

A Winter Scene

Michael Hardman

An Arctic day in England,
Snowman still as statues,
On their monuments; black eyes
Staring out at the snowy fields;
Great hooked noses sticking out,
And smokeless pipes.
A snowman is lifeless with a scarf around his neck;
Footprints around him
Over one another
Meandering through the fields.
A boy is sledding down a hill,
With snowballs hitting him,
He crashes into the snowman,
There's a lump of snow on his head!

Passing Season

Sharon Simmons

Old man winter has been seen around,
Up in the air, and low on the ground,
We do not care as we all sit round the fire
But how long will it take for the old man to tire?

How long will it take for him to tire?
Waiting as the fire burns higher and higher.
In he looks with his tough icicle eye,
His beard hanging down like a long steely tie.

The sun comes out and melts all the snow,
I wonder where it all manages to go.
"Goodbye for now!" we say through the pane
And settle down until he comes again.

Silence is White, Not Golden

Sally Ramsden

Earmuffs of snow
Silences even the dull roar
Of fretting humanity.

For some the silence
Will never ever melt
Into a blackbird's song.

The treacherous black ice
Is always there
Trapping the joyful sounds of life.

Not even a whisper
Will reach those frozen ears
To cheer the lonely soul.

The Daisy Chain

Lesley Kiddell

You placed in the sky a distant star,
You sang of happiness on your guitar,
You ran thro' the park catching leaves with me,
We were so happy and so free.

In Spring by the river watching the rain
You placed round my neck a daisy chain;
In Summer the sun shone for us it seems
As the days wore on those golden dreams.

You held me close when Autumn came,
And the wind was not to blame,
You were there laughing with me
As we sang carols by the Christmas tree.

Now in my hand is the daisy chain,
All withered from lack of rain.
The rain that fell once when you were near
Now becomes one misty tear.

The Dead Tree

Catherine Clough

Enormous elm felled,
Farewell to the shade,
And the whispering sound of the branches.
The grass being less durable is squashed
By the great monster which is laid.
From the distance I see
A curving hollow,
Like a brown cave.
Ivy weaves over the trunk,
Tangled branches lie behind
With their small green leaves;
Cobwebs dangle loosely inside.
A single fungi, dark, orange, brown
Grown on the trunk.
Small animals have made a home
In the secret passage.
Bark peeling off,
Green shading to brown,
Branches bending like fingers,
Beetles and grubs crawling all over,
Sad to see the great tree felled.

What is it All About?

Sally Ramsden

What is it all about?
Asks the child clasping a storybook
Asks the teenager summoned by the Head.

What is it all about?
Asks the lover interrupted in his wooing
Asks the daughter-in-law as the phones rings once
again?

What is it all about?
Asks the thug stopped by the police
Asks the suicidal as he gazes into deep water?

What is it all about?
Asks the scientist as he explores nature
Asks the astronomer as she surveys the stars?

What is it all about?
Asks the philosopher as he studies mankind
Asks the widows and orphans of war?

What is it all about?
Asks the judge trying to see reason
Asks the thoughtful person of his friend?

What is it all about?
Asks Jesus dying on the cross in agony
Asks the heart that desperately needs to know?

Marvellous Creator

Liz Brown

Walking round the garden, what do I see?
Colourful flowers and evergreen trees.
I sit in awe and wonder,
My life's worth, I ponder.
Wonderful Creator, Who has made you and me.

I see small and large birds with wings to fly,
As they glide their way across the sky.
A squirrel darts out from a nearby tree,
Collecting acorns and return to feed.
Across fallen leaves, a field mouse goes rustling by.

Crawling insects and bumble bees.
Amazing how we live with these.
A fat cat prowling nearby,
Ready to pounce on standby,
In awesome wonder, I see my Creator's deeds.

I see my Creator's work at hand.
Small crops grown on the farmer's land.
A rabbit hopping by,
As I try to think why
I am here? I know, to take a stand.

Oh, what a joy to have sunshine and rain.
My Creator gives me life to sustain.
He brought me here for a reason,
Tell others the good news this season.
Before I return to His glory again.

Nightcap Tonic!

Liz Brown

Oh dear! Ali has run out of steam!
Limericked out on the '71 team
Slow down a little dear
Drop back to second gear
Drink nightcap to release odes in your dreams.

(Alison Cookson, (née Mayer) wrote one and sometimes two limericks per day for about a week after the limerick competition was over. On the 7th day she felt limericked out!)

Mags
2007

Envoi

How Much Do You Love Me?

Andrea Fisher

I want to ask you a question, my friend,
Could I have a few minutes of your time?
I wanted to ask you how much you love me,
I was wondering if you were really mine.

I wanted to ask you yesterday,
But you seemed so rushed, so busy
And I would have asked you last night,
But you were more interested in your tv.

I want to ask a question, my friend
I hope that you don't really mind,
I wanted to ask you how much you love me
I am curious as to the answer I'll find.

I wanted to ask you this morning,
But you were talking to somebody else,
And I wanted to ask you last week,
But you were worrying about your health.

I want to ask you a question, my friend
I trust that you don't think I'm prying.
I wanted to ask you how much you love me
Can you answer honestly, without lying?

I would have asked you a while ago,
But you seemed so far away,
And I tried to ask you recently
But you didn't hear me when you prayed.

I really would like to ask you a question
Could you spare me a minute or two?
I just want to know how much you love me,
Is it as much as I love you?

(Jesus Christ stretched his hands out wide)

In Memoriam

Anne Catherine Mazey
1964-1986

Me

Anne Mazey

I want to be Me.

Beholden to no one but me.
Reliant on my instincts and emotions.

Oblivious to the whispering siren calls.
That seductively seek to chain me
To a soulless existence.

Dwelling in the dull conformity
Of life - barren and arid.

I desire the freedom
To be no one but me.

I am Me.

From "Me And Other Poems" by Anne C. Mazey.
Reproduced by kind permission of David and Barbara Mazey.

References

If you would like to know more information about the following charities:

Motor Neurone Disease Association
David Niven House,
10-15 Notre Dame Mews,
Northampton
NN1 2BG
Website: www.mndassociation.org
E-mail: mndconnect@mndassociation.org
Registered Charity No: 294354

Mary Hare Foundation
Arlington Manor
Snelsmore Common
Newbury
Berkshire
RG14 3BQ
Telephone: 01635 244200
Minicom: 01635 244260
Fax: 01635 248019
Website: www.maryhare.org.uk
Registered Charity No: 1048386

National Deaf Children's Society
Head Office
15 Dufferin Street
London
EC1Y 8UR
Tel: 020 7490 8656
Minicom: 020 7490 8656
Fax: 020 7251 5020
Website: www.ndcs.org.uk
Email: ndcs@ndcs.org.uk
Registered Charity No: 1016532

Mary Hare History
Website: www.maryharehistory.org.uk

Further copies of this book can be purchased from
Liz Brown. E-mail: brownliz18@yahoo.co.uk